SKENFRITH'S
LADY OF LETTERS

Skenfrith

SKENFRITH'S
LADY OF LETTERS

The story of Ada Pratlett
with a selection of her poems

KATH HESKETH

Illustrations by Shona Warnes

2003

First published in 1998
by Lapridge Publications

Second edition 2003
published by The Bell at Skenfrith
01600 - 750235

ISBN 1 899290 07 9

British Library Cataloguing in Publication Data
A catalogue record for this book is available
from the British Library

Printed in Great Britain by
Impact Print and Design Limited, Hereford

CONTENTS

FOREWORD

In the 1930s everyone in the Skenfrith area knew Ada Pratlett. She was a welcome visitor to all their homes for she was the local postwoman; a daunting, challenging task. The scattered farms on her daily round were separated by trudging miles and, before she even set out, there was the pre-dawn two-mile walk from Wern Cottage where she lived to the Post Office in Skenfrith to collect her load. Fortunately, by the time of her later move to Cross Cottages in Grosmont, she had managed to save up and buy a bike.

In 1929 Ada had been left a widow with six children; a seventh had died. Her husband George had worked as a stonemason, cleaning and restoring Grosmont Castle after their move to the village from Merthyr Tydfil. George's early death at the age of 42 was, no doubt, precipitated by his lifestyle. He was an alcoholic who would suddenly leave his family for days at a time to tramp the roads. So, financial hardship and bearing the main responsibility for the well-being of her children was already on Ada's agenda. But to face life with no regular income at all and with no Welfare State to cushion the poverty taxed even her reserves of strength.

The post round vacancy seemed Heaven-sent. Despite the prospect of long, hard hours, she did not hesitate. She had feared that the family might, of necessity, be split. Now it could, and would, survive intact.

Then came another stroke of luck. By this time Harry, the eldest son, had become an apprentice gardener at the 'big house', Blackbrook Manor, and Ada was granted the tenancy of Wern Cottage, one of the tied cottages on the estate. It was a humble dwelling, as many of her poems testify; just two tiny rooms downstairs and the same above, with an outside privy and no running water. Water had to be fetched from a well half-a-mile down the road in a wood that stood beside what is now Juniper Cottage.

It's almost impossible to imagine seven people crammed into such a confined space or to envisage the primitive harshness of their daily lives. Yet, Ada's children recall their childhood as 'the happiest time of our lives' and are lavish in their praise of a 'wonderful' mother.

In other circumstances, in another age, Ada would have been acclaimed, not just for her resourceful spirit and triumphs over adversity, but for her intelligence and talents, for she was a lady of letters in more than one sense of the word: she wrote poetry. Some of her poems have survived to form the bulk of this collection, cherished down the years by her daughters, Gladys and Dene. Many have lain tucked away in a drawer far from Skenfrith, on the other side of the world in Australia where Gladys emigrated as a 'ten-pound pom' after the war.

The poems came into my possession by chance, or was it fate? One summer day, eleven years ago, shortly after my husband and I moved into Wern Cottage, we noticed three women peering intently over the hedge. One was Gladys on a nostalgic trip from Australia, the others her sister-in-law and niece. "I lived in this cottage when I was a child," she volunteered. "I can't believe how it's changed."

In they came to inspect and approve the transformation. Thus began a valued friendship, conducted mostly by correspondence, although Gladys has made two subsequent visits. Over the course of time she confessed, somewhat shyly, that both she and her sister Dene wrote poetry, compelled by an unaccountable urge to chronicle their lives in verse. "Somehow it satisfies an inner need. We inherit it from our mother, who was really quite gifted. What I'm trying to do at the moment is to gather all the poems together - mother's, Dene's and mine - to make a family history, for the grandchildren more than anything. As you know, I've got fourteen grandchildren and fourteen great-grandchildren. I hope some of them at least will be curious enough about their roots to want to read it. I don't know if I'll ever even finish it."

"I'd be curious if you do and I'd love to have a copy", I said. Some months later, a copy duly arrived, painstakingly assembled on a word processor which she taught herself to use specially for the purpose, the poems interspersed with old photographs and snippets of family history, all contained within a loose-leaf binder: a true labour of love.

From this massive tome I have culled the poems that are relevant to Skenfrith and locality. They all come straight from the heart, from the sheer joy of creative expression, with no thought of recognition or recompense. The majority of this selection was penned by Ada. Most come across as spontaneous paeans of praise to the everyday sights, sounds and smells of the natural world although, as no work of merit ever emerges fully-formed, they must have been carefully honed. In her busy life, where did Ada find the time and energy? Inevitably, the poems reflect her moods, while darker undertones of personal anguish and hints of domestic turmoil can be detected in many of them.

At the end of the book I have appended a handful of verses written by daughters, Gladys and Dene, for the vivid images they conjure up of the life of an ordinary working family growing up in the 1930s. Their very simplicity has a certain appeal and they are fascinating fragments of vernacular history.

Some of the older members of our community still remember Ada Pratlett, not for her poetry, that was her private retreat, but for her musical prowess. For many years she played the piano at all the dances and social events in the neighbourhood - in Skenfrith Parish Hall, in Grosmont, in Cross Ash. As soon as they were old enough her daughters went along too. They talk animatedly of the enjoyment of these evening jaunts, on foot of course, and this after Ada's long slog delivering the mail.

Ada had been taught the piano from an early age during her childhood at Merthyr Tydfil where her father managed the *Glove and Shears* pub. Apparently, she showed such promise that a visiting American wanted to pay for her to study in America - an invitation promptly scotched by her father who also refused to let her take her beloved piano when, in 1914, she married a local collier, a regular at the pub. Perhaps her parents disapproved of the match and perhaps George was already too fond of a tipple. Playing at the local festivities, then, was the only opportunity she had to practise her skills, as well as providing a welcome supplement to the family's coffers.

Ada Pratlett died in 1943 at the age of 54, shortly after relinquishing the post round. She is buried in Grosmont churchyard in an unmarked grave; a sad and premature ending to a life of promise unfulfilled. The bitter irony is that, after a lifetime of unremitting struggle, spent in the selfless support and care of others, she should die just at the point when she might, at last, have been free to indulge her own dreams.

I like to think that this book will be her modest and belated memorial. I hope it will touch a chord in the hearts of all those who, like Ada Pratlett, draw mental and spiritual solace from the unspoilt beauty of our glorious local countryside which, miraculously, remains much the same as when it was the spring of inspiration for most of her poems, over sixty years ago.

My thanks and appreciation go to Janet and William Hutchings of The Bell at Skenfrith who, inspired by Ada Pratlett's poetry, have kindly funded the reprint of this book.

Kath Hesketh
Wern Cottage

Wern Cottage

Poems

by

Ada Pratlett

Dawn

Grey is the misty morn,
Silent are the hidden hills,
Bright the snaky fern
Down by the crystal rills.
Gold is the flowering lea.
Gold midst the thorny bush
Faintly stirs yon ferny sea,
Awesome the pregnant hush.
Dawn waits with bated breath,
Waits for ecstatic song,
Heralding the chill night's death.
Wake! Wake! ye happy throng!

White shapes move on the hill,
White cots are in the dale,
Castle, church and drowsing mill
Crown'd with the filmy veil.
Eerie is this dripping dawn,
Mystic is her gentle spell,
Upward is my spirit drawn
From its drear and narrow cell.
Hark! where the dark firs tower,
Sweet thro' this poignant hour,
Sing! Sing! ye choir unseen.

This poem describes Skenfrith at dawn, when Ada would arrive to pick up the mail.

The Rural Round

'Tis pleasant to walk on a fair, May morn,
When countless scents from old Earth are borne
On the fitful, elusive breeze
    So warm and sweet.

I pass by the bells of misty blue
Like an azure river winding through.
And the little white tails go frisking
    Across my path.

I look at the fruit trees bloom of snow
'Gainst a background of birch from foot to brow.
Blue column of smoke arising,
    The dog by the gate.

'Tis good to walk when the cold North wind
Puts iron in the blood, brings vigour to the mind.
And the mountain tops of Wales
    Are capped with snow.

On the hill lies the fog, like a blanket below,
Crisp crunches the frost 'neath my feet as I go,
And the cobwebs like jewelled medallions
    Hang from the gate.

And on through the raindrops rhythmic beat,
Through the stinging lash of hail and sleet,
Through the blizzards eerie moan
    I walk my round.

But I like it best when the cold North wind
Puts iron in the blood, brings vigour to the mind
And the mountain tops of Wales
    Are capped with snow.

Whatever the weather, whatever the season, the post round had to be done.

Poppies in the Hedge

I know a hedge, a rank, untidy hedge,
With broken gaps and gateposts jutting out.
A heap of nettles here, some privet there,
A crazy hedge, wild hops entwined about.

It stands before an old, untidy cot,
With blistering walls and broken window panes
But in the hedge and in the cot is that
Which makes me glad to pass that way again.

For, as I round the bend below the gate
A glorious burst of colour greets my eye,
Poppies from palest pink to flaming red
Flaunting exotic beauty to the sky.

Sweet children dance and play about the cot,
Healthy and brown, near naked half the time.
The boys from nether garments flying flags,
Victorious emblems of some hard-fought climb.

Dear urchins! Eyes of dark brown, hazel, blue,
Hair like hostler's brush, a straight unwieldy thatch
But oh! the sweet content, the happy mood,
Look where I will, I do not find their match.

Who sees the weeds? Who sees the poverty
When such as these are patent to the eye?
Were mine the grace to be as these, I would
That ordered care and riches pass me by.

Describing her thoughts on returning from the post round to Wern Cottage.

The Daffodils

That day I walked the fields with heavy heart,
Seeing no hope, almost denying God.
E'en the bleak day was suited to my mood,
Bleak, tho' twas Spring, I cared not where I trod
And found myself upon a bridle path
Leading me up and up through deserted fields,
Offering but scant reward for labour given
And, to the seeking beast, but scanty yields.

The path led to a wood, where all seemed dead,
Which should have pulsed and throbbed with wakening life.
Panting to escape the gloom I reached the top
And resting, gave myself to inner strife.
I saw the mountain tops of distant Wales
Cutting the thin, grey mist that loomed o'er all.
I heard the unseen river's murmuring plaint,
The curlew's lonely, melancholy call.

But lo! I turned my head and there beheld
An unexpected, gladdening sight,
In hundreds, nay in thousands, a smiling bed
Of daffodils, a pool of golden light.
Not all the texts of grave and learned divines
Nor dim cathedrals, low-toned chant and psalm
Could thaw the frozen bands that point the way
To humble faith and hope's enduring balm
As did those happy flowers in that drear spot
That garden blooming in the wilderness.
It seemed the hand of God caressed my brow
Lulling the pain, easing the aching stress.

Returning the way I came I noted things
Unseen before, the slender, silvery wand
Of palm, the tender, uncurled fronds of fern
The aisles of stately larch on either hand.

This poem was inspired by the daffodils, near 'Dawn of Day' , where every Spring they do, indeed, make 'a pool of golden light'.

The Curlew

I heard the curlew calling
Just after break of day.
A melancholy crying
That came from far away.
Though wooded fields were round me
And tilléd fields of corn,
I closed my eyes and lo! I stood
In a grey and desolate morn.
The marshy flats before me
Stretched to a hopeless sky,
The sparse grass dryly rustled
In an oozy creek nearby.
And though I knew no reason
For the grief within my heart,
A poignant yearning filled my soul
For kin who were far apart.

Again, the cry came to me,
A long-drawn, plaintive note
And through the rosy distance
Uneasily it smote.
Though orchards were beside me
And lowed the winding herd,
It seemed I stood midst sandy wastes
Where lived not beast or bird.
The sullen, lowering heavens
Frowned on a heaving sea,
No single gleam of colour
Broke the monotony
And though I knew no reason

For the unrest in my soul
A surge of longing swelled for friends
Whom the bitter years had stole.

I heard the curlew calling
'Twas later in the day
And through the drowsy stillness
He sent his thrilling lay,
A golden chain of music
That linked the Earth with Heaven
A trill so fraught with ecstasy
That my inward soul was riven
I thought of angels winging
I thought of mighty choirs,
Whose song of adoration
Rose like unquenchable fires.
Though I stood in isolation,
Where humans seldom came,
It seemed that Heaven and Earth combined,
In the worship of a name.

The Hills

The green hills 'neath the deep, blue sky
Are fringed with fleecy clouds of light
And darkly green, their shadowy glades
Reach to the purple, brackened height.

The green hills in the moonlit night
Seem to repose in endless rest
And softly beams the silver veil
Shrouding their dim enchanted nest.

The fern steeps, the velvet mounds,
Where wild thyme sheds its fragrance sweet,
The solemn paths of perfumed larch,
The spring of turf beneath my feet.

The woods where ferns and wild flowers grow
Like bright-hued gems amdist the green;
I love these joys of sweet, green hills
Towering above my cottage mean.

Spring is Coming

The spring is coming, tho' eastern winds are blowing
And frost is powdered white on gate and hedge,
The snowdrops clustered thickly, where withered leaves still linger,
Are like a heap of milky pearls, strewn with a careless hand,
And crocuses now push forth their golden spears.

The spring is coming, tho' frozen snow is lying
Upon the hills and 'neath the woodland trees.
The tiny buds are showing upon the naked fruit trees
And in the grey and misty morn, the happy thrush now sings.
The glorious spring is near.
'Tis near! 'Tis near!

Winter

When winter icy stalks the land
With hoary breath and frozen hand
Clutching the last remaining leaves
And blowing its blasts beneath the eaves
Then, oh! for the climb to the snow-clad heights,
Where we view King Frost in all his might
And the glorious night 'neath the glittering stars
And the sound of the wild wind's raging wars.

The height is the hill behind Cross Cottages, Grosmont.

The Road beneath the Crag

Can this be the same place
Which but a few short months ago
Was like an alien, foreign land
Snow everywhere
And cruel, bitter frost?
My echoing footsteps sounded then
Like footsteps in a dungeon
As I passed by the ancient wall
Where, so legend has it, a ghostly spectre
Climbs o'er at midnight.
For myself, I've never seen the gentleman
Though oft I passed that way
At midnight and later still!

I had to stoop to pass beneath the boughs,
Bending 'neath their heavy load of ice, stood up
Like stiff, fantastic ornaments
Within the woods which partly clothe the hill.
Huge boughs and tops of trees
Came crashing down
With a harsh, rending grind,
Like giants felled to the earth
By the club of an ancient foe.
From afar, it might have been a graveyard,
Strewn with the whitened bones
Of prehistoric monsters
That had travelled there to die.

A thin, depressing mist loomed over all
Nothing stirred save the poor sheep
Seeking hungrily amidst the hedge

For withered grass and leaves.
A ghostly silence
Except upon the hill, whence came,
Those strange, continuous crashings,
An alien place, uncanny, unreal.

But now betwixt the heaps
Of rotting wood and tangled briar
Bloom sweet, late primroses.
And where the wood lies thickest
And where the thorns most sharp
The finest blossoms grow.
Here do the lovely bluebells seem
Like floating pools of misty blue
And wild, luxuriant undergrowth
Creeps o'er the fallen trees.
The bluebells stir,
Faint ripples passing through them.
Are they brushed by the silken train of a gown?
Do they make obeisance to a tiny queen
Unseen by mortal eye?

No graveyard now, a roofless church
A sanctuary
With columns of wood instead of stone.
And God's own choir unseen
Pouring its sweet, unending praise to Heaven.
My footsteps echo faintly
As I pass the ancient wall
But now they sound like footsteps in a cloister.

*The 'ancient wall' with its 'ghostly spectre' is located on the road to Grosmont,
just beyond White House Farm.*

O! Green Hill

O! green hill 'neath the deep, blue sky
Fringed with the fleecy clouds of light.
How happy I, if I could die
With my dimmed gaze upon thy height
And happier still that I may live
With my clear gaze upon thy brow,
Thy gentle slopes, thy nestling cots
And my heart filled with joy, as now.

Dark are the glades upon thy breast
O! green hill in the moonlit night.
And on thy dim, enchanted crest
How softly beams the silver light.
And splashing, gurgling, gliding on
Around thy foot, the river sings
By lichened roof, by ivied barn
Past where the echoing axes ring.

And when, at eve, the heavens draw nigh
Merging with thee in quiet embrace,
While from the West the golden sky
Reflects its glory on thy face,
'Tis then I climb the ferny steeps
And pace with slow and reverent tread
Those sombre paths, thro' perfumed larch,
While sighs the evening breeze o'erhead.

O! solemn paths thro' perfumed larch
Priests nor confessional none should need

To ease his soul of sins that parch
Of utterance mean and meaner died.
For here he cast aside the cloak
Of paltry, smug hypocrisy.

But stands, abashed in shaméd awe
Of Nature's grand sincerity.

A Prayer

To hear the first bird call,
A sweet and twittering note
That wakes a hundred echoes
From each feathered songster's throat,
Till on a stream of rapturous song
My wondering soul is swept along,
Up to the rosy gates of Heaven
Up to the throne of God

To mount the hill at morn,
To tread the scented way,
Where gleam a million jewels
To watch the sudden ray
Leap from the golden, gorse-clad height,
To see the beaming shaft of light
Pierce the grey hill of timid dawn
And tint her shimmering garb.

To hear this, to see this
Dear Lord, to me is the soul of bliss.
Oh! let me walk where the green boughs meet
And keep my path from the pavéd street.

To walk through gentle rain
When from her robe of green
The Earth shakes forth her incense,
When dust smells sweet and e'en
The stony road a fragrance gains.
'Tis then the quiet, ancient lanes,
Banked by the sombre, slender firs

A perfumed cloister seems.
To sit at dewy eve
When skies are quiet and grey
And green hills stand out clearly,
When scent of new-mown hay
And sound of busy mower fills
The little world within the hills
Slowly and quietly falls the night
And labour's earned its rest.

To do this, to see this
Dear Lord to me is the soul of bliss.
Oh! let me walk where the green boughs meet
And keep my path from the pavéd street.

Skenfrith Church

Journey's End

I get a pleasant smile at journey's end
A kindly welcome and a cup of tea
A jest, a chat, here for a little while
I sit apart and rest carefree

This poem refers to Barn Farm, the last call on Ada's round. It belonged to the in-laws of Enid Prosser who, at the age of 93, still enjoys life at White House Farm on the Grosmont road.

Grosmont Castle

Grosmont Castle (1918)

Grey stones and dark green ivy,
A close-flecked sky above,
Daws chattering, soft liquid chatterings,
Quiet peacefulness I love.
The moat a place of beauty,
Where fern and bluebells grow,
The hawthorn's cloud of whiteness,
Dark purple fruit of sloe.

The walls of crumbling beauty
Set in a sylvan sea,
The lichen in the crannies
Weave a witchery.

Fain would I linger longer,
Where stones have the power to speak.
Fain would I sit and wonder
At the strength of the ruined keep.

Grey stones and dark green ivy,
A solemn hush o'er all.
Faint rustlings, soft breezes stirring
The tall grass by the wall.
The clang of the village anvil
Makes homely music meet
For this ancient stately grandeur,
Where the ghosts of the past retreat.

Grosmont Castle (1930)

Reluctantly I leave thee,
Slowly I pace the sward,
Each lingering look of longing
Brings me a rich reward.
Yon gleams the silver ribbon,
Aloft the fern-topped brow,
The wood of tangled glory
Veils the deep steep below.

When a lonely soul I wander
Through the city's crowded hours
This scene will rise before me
At the scent of homely flowers.
With a rush of pain I'll see thee,
When faint is borne to me
The strains of old-time music
In simple harmony.

When ghostly glides the river
And early through the gloom
The giant ships of commerce
Like shapeless spectres loom.
I shall see the mists that shroud thee
Grey as the ancient tower,
When the master brush of Autumn
Has tinted this sylvan bower.

This poem was written when Ada had been recently widowed and was about to move from Grosmont to Wern Cottage, Skenfrith. The future was uncertain. Did she fear that she might one day be forced by circumstances to live in a city?

Snow Clouds

White clouds - snow clouds - banked in massive piles,
Sweeping, creeping at the North wind's wiles.
A vast array of spearmen marching o'er the plain,
A line of shrouded mourners, heads bowed in pain.

A snow queen's ice-built castle, poised on sharp-toothed crags,
Leaping in the foreground, a herd of antlered stags.
O'er there, a grand cathedral, spreading hills behind,
I hear the rolling organs, played by the mighty wind.

Bright clouds - cold clouds - massed tier on tier,
Ranging, changing, now afar, now near,
A densely-packed arena, rampant beasts enclose,
A couch of snow inviting treacherous repose.

A lone, deserted city, built upon a hill,
Rooftop piled on rooftop, a street that's never still,
Now changing, now dividing, clear-cut, brilliant, straight,
A blue and radiant pathway leading up to Heaven's gate.

Hurrying, scurrying, pouring, leaping over the hill they come
Whirling, twisting, lingering, marching, crowding the wintry dome.
What is the fear that drives them fleeing from verge to verge,
Dancing fantastic measures, puppets to wild wind's dirge?

See the white glory fading. Hark to the pipe grown shrill
A shrill yet mournful cadence, a high-pitched sobbing trill.
Gone is the fancied castle, gone the figures of woe,
See now a restless ocean, grey waves with crests of snow.

The gathering snowflakes rustling fall,
Laying a white sheet over all,
Bowing the branch of a fir tree tall
Painting a weird light on the wall,
Hushing the blackbird's fleeting call,
Holding the eye in beauty's thrall.
Faster, faster, blurring the sight,
Till nought but a whirling veil of white
Dances 'tween eye and glooming fall.

A Christmas Wish

When sweet bells chime on Christmas morn
A tuneful, merry song of joy
A heartfelt wish I send to you
For all that's good without alloy.
O! bear it ye bells now high, now low
Far o'er the white and sparkling snow.

When thro' the crisp and starry night
The hymn of peace swells rich and clear,
I wish for you a joyous time,
Good fellowship and love, my dear.
O! flash it far ye stars on high
Far thro' the glittering, trackless sky.

When, in the quiet of friendly night
I think of Christmastides long flown,
I pray that you may know the joys
And miss the griefs that I have known.
O! hear me in Heaven thou child of love
Grant me this prayer from thy throne above.

A New Year Greeting

Here's to you, friend, thro' good and ill
May the goddess of luck be with you still,
Softening the ill, till good it beseems,
Enhancing the good beyond your dreams.
May the fates bring you love where'er you list
And only sweet memories of those you have kissed.
May they bring you wealth and wisdom, too,
To wisely spend. May you never rue
The loss of a friend, or triumph a foe.
May stout hearts be with you where'er you go.

'Tis in My Heart

I think of you my darling
When palely creeps the dawn across my chamber
And wearily I rise to sordid care.
My soul, like bird released, sweeps up in rapture
    At thoughts of you.

I think of you my darling,
When on the distant hill the sun marks out
A field of yellow corn amidst the green.
Athwart my heart, like zephyrs sweetly whispering,
    Come thoughts of you

I long for you my darling,
When through the spangled curtain of the rain,
I glimpse the iridescent arc of beauty
And when the sun, his teardrops spent, beams warmly,
    I see your smile

I hear your voice my darling
Plainly I hear it on wild, wind-swept morns,
I hear it in the sheltered ancient barn
Methinks that you are near. Then comes the knowledge
    'Tis in my heart.

'Tis in my heart my darling,
Bidding me fix my hope upon the heights,
Telling me there's beauty o'er the hilltop,
    If I but climb.

Long after she was widowed, Ada was courted by a bachelor farmer, who lived in
a farm on her post round. They met socially when she played the piano at the

local dances and after they finished at 11pm, he would escort her and the girls home. Eventually, he proposed marriage but she refused, although it would have solved her money problems, as he was financially comfortable. Perhaps she feared the effect upon the children, perhaps she still loved her husband, despite the stormy relationship. So, it is not known whether this poem is addressed to her late husband or her new suitor.

Night

The still, grey skies are resting on the hills,
Those ancient, dark green hills that stand out clear
And night is softly closing in.
Upon their slopes faint, twinkling lights appear
That point the way to lonely cots and farms.

And high upon yon wood one solit'ry light
Is moving slowly o'er the dark hill's face
Perchance some weary labourer plodding home,
For now doth weary labour earn its rest.

The darkness comes, the hills have lost their shape
And are but dim, mysterious masses lit
By stars remote in Heaven's firmament.
And clearly comes the unseen river's song,
Murmuring its placid way through brackened fields.

The swooping bats are darting for their prey,
The frogs are croaking in the stagnant pool.
Oh! sweet the perfumed breath of perfect night,
Each tiny noise a joy that in the day
Is lost amidst the battlefield of life.

Bury Me Not

Bury me not 'neath the churchyard's mould
Away from the blue or white of the day,
From wreathed, grey mists o'er ancient hills
And the faint, sweet scent of creamy may.

Oh! lay me not down with orderd pomp,
'Neath the smooth green sward of a grim town's plot,
Where sculptured urn and granite stone
Mount a cold guard o'er the body's rot.

Not e'en by the green-treed, hoary lane
Near the racing mill and the fields of corn,
Where mossy stones lean aslant with age
And the sweet bells chime on Christmas morn.

Carry my ashes to yonder hill,
To yon far-off hill with its ferny brow
And scatter them wide and scatter them free
O'er tilth and fallow and forest bough.

And may some rest in the deep, still wood,
Where the sly fox stays in his headlong flight
And the sun shines through on the moist, green floor,
Like a shimmering, liquid lake of light.

And may some rest by the busy brook,
With boulders strewn where the grey trout leap,
Where white mist curls on the morning air
And dappled shade lies, where kine drink deep.

Oh! take them and bear them, thou sweet, free breeze,
Where wild creatures linger, where swayeth the trees,
Where whispereth dark firs, when the swift clouds race,
Where smooth glide the shadows across the hill's face.

Alas, Ada's wish was not granted. She is buried in the churchyard of St. Nicholas, Grosmont, in an unmarked grave.

Grosmont Churchyard

Poems

by

Dene Watson
(Ada's younger daughter)

Little Cross
My First Home

I remember days gone by, when I was just a child,
The little cottage where we lived, with flowers growing wild,
The hill that rose behind us, the valley down below.
In Spring the fields were flooded from the swollen river's flow.

I loved to roam the meadow, with its myriad of flowers, .
Run barefoot through the long grass, spend many happy hours.
In summertime I'd climb the hill, where fern and bluebell grow,
See foxgloves in the hedgerows, taste the bitterness of sloe.

From the door I would look as far as eye could see,
To wooded slopes of Garway Hill, where deer would wander free.
Across the hillside I'd watch shadows come and go,
Their ghostly shapes would disappear, to where I did not know.

I'd walk the leafy lane and smell the heady scent of May
In nearby field, the farmer turned his crop of new-mown hay.
I'd hear the cuckoo calling, his message to convey,
'My visit's short, so hurry up, I have not long to stay'.

I paused a while to contemplate the beauty of this spot,
A feeling crept up over me, which I have ne'er forgot.
And in the years that followed, when'er I felt the same
I'd think about the time I walked along that country lane.

Wern Cottage - Home No. 2

My second home was where I spent my childhood years till ten.
We came here when my dad died, to start our lives again.
My mum was left with five of us to bring up on her own.
A missing sister, far away, who lived with Gran on loan.

To make ends meet my mother took a job delivering mail,
Each morning she would leave the house, come sunshine, rain or hail,
She did this for the next ten years, her life was one long toil
But at the end, she'd look at us and think it all worthwhile.

In springtime, I would waken to the pigeons softly cooing
A sure sign that the time had come for them to start a-wooing.
I'd listen to the blackbird's song, the notes so pure and clear,
Serenading to his mate, who waited somewhere near.

I'd watch the early morning mist arising from the river
Where later on, when sun was warm, the dragonflies would hover.
The sudden plop of stickleback as they darted to and fro
Their iridescent colours seen in gentle water's flow.

My sister came to live with us, together we would play.
We paddled in the sunlit brook and on its banks would lay.
We climbed the trees, swung on the boughs, picked chestnuts in the fall,
At Christmas time to have some treats, we loved the most of all.

Two special skills my mother had, the piano she could play.
From early childhood she had learnt and practised every day.
An accomplished player at thirteen was what she then became,
She did so well, she could have added letters to her name.

In local village hall we went to listen to her play,
And join in country dancing to pass the night away.
These happy evenings spent by us years later I'd recall
And number them among the things that I loved best of all.

The other gift my mother had was writing poetry,
Much later on her poems now are kept by Glad and me.
This legacy she left with us we will always treasure.
Looking back, the words she wrote have given us much pleasure.

The years have gone but memory's strong of things that used to be,
The happy days I spent here were all a part of me.
I would not change one little bit these things I hold most dear,
The only thing I would have wished was that my dad be here.

view from Wern Cottage

Broad Oak - Home No. 3

When I was ten, we moved again, things were different now,
Two brothers gone, my sister too, not the same somehow.
Gran and Grandad shared our home; I sensed the discord here,
My days were not so happy, my thoughts were tinged with fear.

What brought it on I'll never know but one day things went wrong
Grannie jumped into the well, I thought that she had gone.
Somehow Grandad fished her out, for help I had to go,
He managed to revive her but recovery was slow.

When Gran was on her feet again, they found another place.
It made things easier for Mum and gave her breathing space.
We kept our eyes on both of them for many months to come
But in the end poor Grannie died, her life's work had been done.

Not long after Grannie died, we're on the move once more,
Back to where we started from, this time to house next door
My sister Glad was still away, in France's foreign land,
My brother, in the Air Force, was stationed close at hand.

My eldest brother in the army serving overseas.
War was looming ever closer, people felt unease.
A stroke had struck poor Grandad down, his mental state had gone,
We kept him with us for a while but nothing could be done.

War had come but in this spot it touched us not one bit.
Sister Glad was called back home, had to make a quick exit.

Another brother, Philip, on nearby farm was working.
Life went on just the same, no hidden dangers lurking.

My sister left our home once more, to be a mental nurse.
No news from eldest brother, things were getting worse.
To ease my mother's worry, I wrote to army base.
After waiting weeks for news, we still could find no trace.

For youngest brother, George, and I, our schooldays now are over.
Time to start our working lives, a well-earned rest for mother.
But as so often happens, when someone calls a halt,
Mum's health began to fail her, body's organs were at fault.
I worked for eighteen months and then my job just had to go,
I came back home to care for Mum, her health was very low.
She spent some months in hospital, was better for a while
But somehow in her heart she knew she'd reached the final mile.

One cold November evening my mother passed away.
A fine example to us all, in life she did portray.
I'd like to think that I possess some attributes of hers,
So that I, too, can leave behind some strong memories through the years.

At a very young age, Gladys was sent to live with her maternal grandparents in the Glove and Shears pub in Merthyr Tydfil, probably to ease the pressures of overcrowding and poverty. She did not return to live with the family until her mother moved into Wern Cottage in 1930, by which time her ageing grandmother was unable to care for her competently. Then, when she was fifteen, she was sent to France as a nanny-cum-English teacher-cum-skivvy to a local family, who were going there to live. She had to return home in 1939, just before the outbreak of war. Harry, the eldest brother, survived the war and came back to live in Skenfrith. The move from Broad Oak was literally back to where they started - Cross Cottages at Grosmont.

Grosmont

Poems

by

Gladys Price
(Ada's elder daughter)

Skenfrith

Wern Cottage was a poor man's home,
Two rooms downstairs and up.
The old stone floors, no taps were there,
And candles in a cup.
We broke the ice to wash ourselves,
Drank water from a well
But life was rich in memories
That I have lived to tell.

Our Dad had died two years before,
Mum took the place of two.
She ruled the roost o'er all we kids,
No cheek! And lies taboo!
Dear God, how I respected her,
I knew she did her best.
To rear six imps without a Pa
That gave no cause for jest!

She delivered mail to all the farms
In sun and snow and rain.
For years she walked so many miles
And never did complain.
At country dance and social
She played piano too
To boost the family finance
Was all that she could do.

I see the cottage garden,
Haphazard, growing wild.
The damson and the pear trees,

With fruit to please a child.
The brilliant, coloured poppies,
The ragged, broken hedge,
Gate swinging on its hinges
Beside the dirt path's edge.

And sliding down the wash-house roof,
With Mum away from home,
Our feet all black, our bottoms, too,
From dust and earth's dark loam.
And carol singing in the snow,
When Christmas Eve came round,
With tingling toes and fingers
From Jack Frost on the ground.

I swung from trees as monkeys do
And knew no fear at all
And rode an ancient bicycle
And suffered many a fall.
My sister and my brothers,
We carted wood for Mum
To cook our food and wash our clothes,
No fancy stove, like some.

Through buttercups and daisies
Knee-deep we walked in Spring,
Midst swarms of bees and dragonflies
And listened to birds sing.
Tasted watercress from bubbling streams,
Had picnics on the bank,
Skimmed pebbles through the water
And watched them till they sank.

Blackbrook Estate, Mum's landord's home,
The Herrings bided there.
My brother, Harry, worked for them,
For they were gentry fair.
He tilled the ground and sowed the seed,
Girl Guides Miss Herring led.
Her appendix burst, it was too late,
At twenty she was dead.

The day we four played tracking,
Dene, Lip, George and I,
The game was so engrossing,
My! - how the time did fly.
When Mother called us to our lunch
No notice did we take.
Four very hungry children,
No meal we could partake.

Then Dene and I one day we went
To Skenfrith's only shop.
Instead of walking home again
We stayed for 'village hop'.
'Twas late at night we started off,
Mum met us on the way.
The biggest belting I received,
Half-way through hedge I lay.

I ran along inside the field.
Mind seethed with discontent.
To run away, I vowed I would,
As 'gainst the gate I leant.
But gradually I realised

How futile that would be,
I set off home and then, behold
Mum came to look for me.

No word we spoke as, side by side,
We walked along the road.
But I could sense her anger'd gone
It lessened my mind's load.
I did not hang around downstairs
But went up straight to bed,
Realizing truly then,
Soonest mended, if least said.

I walked to Norton Cross to school,
A good three miles each day.
From there I passed exam to High,
Down Abergavenny way.
Two miles to walk, twelve miles by bus,
A mile the other end,
To leave the bus, the night pitch dark,
It drove me round the bend.

'Lip' was brother Philip

A Tribute to My Sister

I'm thinking back along the years
To when we both were small,
To the early 1930s
When Wern Cottage was our all.
'Twas such a tiny, little home,
Of rooms it boasted four.
Outside a lean-to wash-house,
Throughout was old stone floor.

No windows were there at the back
'Twas built smack against the ground.
I suppose it kept the cold at bay
When winter came around,
We slept with Mam, three to a bed,
It was the best that she could do.
We knew no other kind of life
So had no cause to rue.

Mam delivered mail to all the farms
In sun and rain and sleet.
No car, no bike, no transport,
Just used her own two feet.
We kids walked down to Norton School,
About a mile or more;
Two classrooms housed the lot of us,
From fourteen down to four.

Harry was a gardener,
On Blackbrook land he toiled,
While Fred became the scholar,

His hands with ink, not earth, were soiled.
'Twixt Fred and I a four-year gap,
Then Lip and you and George;
With neighbours few and far between
A bond we did truly forge.

The day we all played tracking
You three as well as I,
So engrossed were we, we heeded not
Mam's call to lunch nearby.
We thought we were hard-done by
When she made us go without,
And moaned and groaned behind the shed;
Harry grinned and pursed his mouth.

We used to climb the apple trees
Before the fruit was ripe,
The tell-tale signs - pan full of worms
And our stomachs full of gripe!
The big beech tree above 'The Lodge',
Just down the road a way,
Its ivy-covered branches
Would hold the world at bay.

On the oaks inside the orchard
We'd swing from branches high
Like monkeys hooked by knee or foot,
We'd make our bodies fly.
And talking to the navvies,
Who on their shovels leant
And from this quite often pastime
Their bodies were real bent!

Miss Herring gave us dollies
And knitting things beside.
The old tin shack, so squat and low,
We had to crawl inside.
The knitting books were 'baby' size
The dollies rather small.
Somehow we managed to knit those clothes
To fit, with pattern and all.

To boost the family's finance
Mam played piano too
At social and at country dance
She'd accompany villagers true.
And sliding down the wash-house roof
With Mam away from home,
Our feet were black, our bottoms, too,
Garnered from earth's dark loam.
And then across the fields we'd go
Watching the flight of the swallow,
Beside the brook with watercress
We'd picnic in a hollow.

The blue and golden dragonflies,
Sun glinting midst the leaves,
Breeze soughing through the grasses,
Bird song and hum of bees.
The grand old William pear tree,
The juicy fruit so gold,
The dozens lying on the ground
For the wasps paradise untold.
And carol singing in the snow,
When Christmas Eve came round,
E'en so, from that so long ago,
I still feel joy abound.

Then waiting for that Sunday feast
Our bellies rumbling loud,
Those great big plates of bread and jam
That vanished like a cloud.
The years have dimmed the memories,
We're both of us growing old.
Mam, Harry, Fred, George and Lip
Have relinquished Life's heavy load.
Our paths took us so far apart.
You stayed, I came 'down under'
But that sense of belonging has never gone,
Our love for each other, still a wonder.

These reminiscences of Gladys, written in Australia in April 1993 when she was 72, reveal the rare depth of feeling of a close-knit family - a legacy which would, perhaps, have been more satisfying to Ada Pratlett than all her poetry.